# Why Wait?

## by Rob Quillen

Headline Books, Inc.
Terra Alta, WV 26764

# Why Wait?

by
Rob Quillen

copyright ©2012 Rob Quillen

To order additional copies of the book, or to contact the author:

Headline Books, Inc.
P O Box 52
Terra Alta, WV 26764

www.HeadlineBooks.com
www.RobQuillen.com

ISBN-13: 978-0-938467-23-6

*Cover Photos:*
*Never forget by Terry.Runion the Photographer*
*9-11 Composition by Bruce Roff*

Library of Congress Control Number: 2011934181


Quillen, Rob
 Why Wait?/ by Rob Quillen

ISBN-13: 978-0-938467-23-6
1. September 11, 2001 2. U.S. History. 3. New York City.
Non-Fiction

PRINTED IN THE UNITED STATES OF AMERICA

*Dedication*

This book is dedicated to some very special people in my life.

First and foremost, to my mom. You taught me to overcome any obstacle that I would ever face in life. I still miss you each and every day that passes.

To Abigail and John, may all of your dreams in life come true. I hope that no matter what you do in life, you choose a path in life that you can make a difference in people's lives and that you can make other people's dreams come true every day.

# Foreword

## By Marty Smith

I am a staunch believer in the Human Spirit, sometimes to an unrealistic degree. Life's fickleness taught me young to celebrate the good in people, and to try my very best to tolerate the not-so-good. My own personal failures accentuated that approach.

I count God's blessings and I am cognizant of His expectation that I pay them forward. That approach has encouraged ridicule at times. But it has never failed me.

Ultimately, The Golden Rule prevails over any criticism it may foster, because, in my mind, treating others as you'd appreciate being treated fosters self-confidence, and self-confidence allows a man the willingness to take chances in the name of the greater good. It also allows a man the willingness to be genuinely happy for others. They, then, are apt to be happy for him.

Sometimes Faith pulls you in a direction you may find curious, and therefore resist. But in this brief life you must sometimes let faith be your guide. You must take it by the hand with the enthusiasm to be led where it leads.

Otherwise 'What If' presides over 'I did.' Few things in life are as fulfilling as 'I did.'

This happened to me once back in September 2001, by way of a random email from a pool of dozens of random emails. As a columnist for NASCAR.com in the pre-social networking world, I received countless emails daily from outspoken fans across the country, just looking for an outlet to voice concerns and opinions and ideas. These days folks take to Twitter or Facebook to offer real-time feedback and analysis to public figures. In 2001, they solicited the help of media types like me with public email addresses.

After the September 11, 2001 terrorist attacks on the World Trade Center and the Pentagon, NASCAR, like many leagues, chose to postpone its event the following weekend. The race was to be run that weekend in Loudon, New Hampshire, but instead would be pushed to Thanksgiving weekend.

Afterward, folks wrote me to commend the decision – as if I had any say in it – and to grieve and share personal thoughts on America's darkest hour. During my lifetime, our country had never been so unified. While negotiating the sea of feedback, I happened upon an email from a gentleman named Rob Quillen.

Quillen was an ardent Jeff Gordon fan, and we had corresponded sporadically in the past about Gordon's various on-and-off track exploits. But this one was different.

This one was eerie. This one was hair-raisingly personal. This one claimed he needed my help to grant a wish so far-fetched it couldn't be false. If it were, it would be the cruelest and sickest of pranks. And as I read it I realized – this one would require taking Faith by the hand, and the willingness to be lead to its destination. This one required belief in the Human Spirit.

Quillen told the story that he had on September 10, 2001, flown alongside a gentleman named Jason Dahl. Dahl was a pilot, and the following day would fly United Flight 93 from Newark, New Jersey to San Francisco, California.

The men shared commonalities. Both were family men and both were Gordon fans. As the hours passed the conversation grew more personal, and Dahl told Quillen about his epileptic son, Matt, who was also a Gordon fan. Matt wanted badly to attend a NASCAR race and meet Gordon, and that hope became Jason Dahl's mission.

Then Flight 93 crashed in a remote Pennsylvania field on September 11, 2001.

Dahl is an American Hero of the highest order. He and his comrades triumphed over evil in the greatest and most-selfless of sacrifices.

And when the realization hit Quillen that his new friend was aboard that plane, Jason's mission became Rob's mission: Find a way to get Matt Dahl to the race track and some way, any way, meet his hero.

Quillen's email to me that day was the first step in the lengthy chain of events this book details that, all said, is nothing short of miraculous.

The second step in that chain of events?

Faith in the Human Spirit.

# Introduction

Imagine sitting next to a loved one lying in a deathbed with twenty-four hours to live. Imagine the pain and sorrow. What would you say? Would you ask personal or private questions? Would you share stories or even secrets with each other? What emotions would you experience? What do you think your loved one is thinking about right now? Would you ask the question, "You have only twenty-four hours left to live, is there anything you have always wanted to do but never did?"

With twenty-four hours left to live, odds are, there are not too many dreams that can still be fulfilled.

Now, picture the same person sitting next to you knowing you will get to spend another twenty years with him or her. What would you say? Would you ask very personal or private questions? Would you share stories and maybe even share a secret? What emotions would you have?

Would you ask the question, "If you had only twenty-four hours left to live, is there anything you have always wanted to do but haven't done yet?"

With twenty years to look forward to, the odds are good that you could help make many dreams become a reality for your friend or loved one.

Why do we treat someone with twenty-four hours left to live differently than someone who we assume has another twenty years with us?

This book will show you my journey and an experience through life of how, once I finally realized and understood the meaning of truly connecting with another person, dreams can be fulfilled before it is too late.

Everyone has a hidden layer inside. It is our personal threshold into our heart and dreams. It is up to you to reach that inner layer of everyone you know before it is too late. It is up to you to cross that threshold to ensure that when your friends and loved ones pass away, they are left with no regrets and no unfulfilled dreams.

At the end of this book, I hope you are asking yourself one very simple question.

Why Wait?

# Chapter 1
## September 10, 2001

In 2001, I was enjoying a fantastic sales career with Automated Data Processing (ADP) and traveling was a big part of my job. This particular week's travels had me going to New York for some sales meetings.

In the weeks prior, all of us reps were told that we would be split up into three different groups and travel to various cities for these meetings. One group was going to New York City, one group to San Francisco and another group was heading to Chicago. My boss called me and told me I was going to the New York meeting. I questioned him several times on why I was not going to the Chicago meeting when Chicago was only an hour flight for me. I could save the company at least two nights worth of hotel stay, save money on the airfare, etc. I did not win the argument, so on September 10th, 2001, I drove myself to the airport in Lincoln, Nebraska to fly to New York City.

When I checked in for my flight, I was told my seat could not be confirmed as the flight was oversold, but I should go to the gate and wait for announcements. Upon arriving at my gate, the gate attendant was already yelling into the PA system. Several different times, she asked volunteers to get off of the flight only to promise, "You will be placed on the next flight and you will arrive in your destination city as soon as possible," blah, blah, blah. A couple of people volunteered, but they still needed a few more people. After several minutes of no other volunteers, I heard my name over the PA system. I went to the counter where I was told that I was taken off my flight. I questioned the gate agent why I was the one who had to get off the flight. Her response was nothing less than classic.

"Well, Mr. Quillen, our records indicate you were the last person to purchase a ticket for this flight. As a result, you are the first person who has to be removed from the flight."

I did not say anything at first, especially with the thoughts that were racing through my mind. *Really, who in the world came up with this brilliant plan?*

I was told I was being rescheduled on a flight from Omaha through Denver and into Newark, New Jersey. My original flight was from Lincoln through Chicago into JFK.

At this point, I am still dealing with the same person who explained how I was chosen to be removed from the flight, so I guess the answer to my next question should have been expected.

I asked her if she knew I was not in Omaha, Nebraska but rather in Lincoln, Nebraska and that she was rebooking me on a flight that was leaving from Omaha.

"Of course I do, Mr. Quillen. That is why we are giving you a free bus ride to Omaha."

"Of course, why wouldn't you?" I said.

Normally this type of travel change would not be that big of a deal for me, but I was heading into New York City a day early, prior to my meetings, to hang out with some of my friends who were flying in for the same meeting. We had the whole afternoon and evening planned. We were going to have a great dinner in Times Square.

Now that my plans changed, I was more than frustrated because I was the last person to buy a ticket for the flight. I was even more annoyed because I elected to wear jeans and a polo shirt instead of my normal business suit I usually wore on the plane. I always wear a suit on flights because I hate leaving a suit in my luggage. Nothing makes me more frustrated than a wrinkled suit. I wore casual clothes to go have some fun, now my suit was in my suitcase getting all kinds of wrinkles.

The bus ride to Omaha and the flight to Denver were both uneventful. After a short layover in Denver, I boarded my flight to Newark. Traveling as much as I did at the time, I was upgraded to the first row behind first class. I asked if I could be upgraded to first class, but the customer service rep told me that first class was full.

While sitting on the plane waiting to take off, several of us noticed the door to the airplane was still open but no other passengers were boarding the plane. The door remained open for several more minutes before some of the passengers arbitrarily started moving seats on their own. I was already in the seat that I wanted, business class, seat A, by the window.

After a couple of minutes, two gentlemen came and sat next to me. Shortly after that, a flight attendant came and told them they had to go back to their original seats because they were waiting for some more passengers from another flight to arrive. They moved and shortly after that a handful of people came aboard. The last person on the plane sat in my row, two seats over—seat C.

The door finally closed and the normal preflight stuff started. Here is how to put your life jacket on, here is how to exit the plane, etc. To be honest with you, as much as I travel, I was not paying attention to anything as I have seen the demonstration way too many times to mention. Little did I know this was going to be the last normal thing I heard for the next twenty-four hours, thirty days, and five years or maybe for even the rest of my life.

While the preflight video was going, a flight attendant came over and handed my new rowmate a cold beer. I looked at him and said, "You are either someone very important or you are dating her, but either way, well done."

He laughed and said, "Neither, I am a pilot and I am dead heading to Newark tonight. I have the 8:15 a.m. flight to San Francisco tomorrow."

We shook hands and he introduced himself to me. "Jason Dahl, nice to meet you.

"Rob Quillen, nice to meet you, Jason," as we shook hands.

# Chapter 2

## Flight 7114 Denver, Colorado to Newark, New Jersey

As I have said before, airline travel was very normal to me. Like most traveling professionals, I believe airplane time is a little gift from God. I am finally forced to sit for three or four hours and get stuff done, such as expense reports, catching up on emails, reports that I am behind on, etc. Other than a short pleasantry or two, I never speak to anyone who is sitting next to me. Again, it is my time. While I will usually give my rowmate the respect of not putting my iPod ear buds in my ears right away, if the person sitting next to me starts talking about anything, out comes the iPod. Especially if they start to talk to me about their vacation plans and their kid keeps turning on and off the overhead light. I don't care that your family is heading to Disney World —I don't want to sing any Disney songs along with you and your kids. It is my time.

Flight 7114 was going to change this part of me forever.

Jason, my new row mate, asked me if I worked for Jeff Gordon. I remember thinking, *what kind of question is that?* Then I remembered I was in casual clothes and wearing a polo shirt representing Jeff Gordon.

"No, I am just a big Jeff Gordon and NASCAR fan," I said.

"My son and I are big fans too, in fact we just talked about going to a race."

I knew right then I was not going to get any work done for the rest of this flight. I have many passions in life, but most of all I love talking NASCAR to fellow fans. NASCAR racing is a huge part of my life. I have not missed even one lap of a race, practice or qualifying, in over twenty years. I think the word passion fits well when I describe what it means to me, but that may be an understatement.

At this point, I could have easily ended the conversation right there just like I had a thousand times before. I could have made a couple of more NASCAR comments, maybe even asked another question or two, then ended it right there. I could have turned on my laptop and drifted away into work for the next few hours.

> At this point, I could have easily ended the conversation...

For some reason, my mind told me to keep the conversation going. Maybe it was the long day I had, or maybe I thought a NASCAR conversation over a beer would make my day better. Maybe it was something else.

"Really, what track are you guys thinking about going to?" I said.

"We are thinking about hitting Talladega for the spring race next year," Jason responded.

"I have been to a lot of races over the years, but I have never been there, but that is a race I want to go and see. I love the speed of the cars and I love how close they race the entire day," I responded.

"Yeah, my son thinks that Talladega has some real action so he wants to go," Jason said.

"Well, 'Dega can give us some amazing wrecks from time to time. If you guys want to see real action, Talladega would be the place to go. Either that or Daytona or even Bristol, either way, you guys will be set."

I asked Jason what NASCAR driver he and his son followed. He did not hesitate when he pointed at my shirt and said, "Gordon."

He asked me about races I attended, my opinions of different drivers, different exciting races, and his plans to get his son, Matt, to a race soon.

For the next three hours, Jason and I started a conversation that would change my life. We got past the, "What do you do for a living Rob, and how long have you been flying, Jason?" questions and had a three hour conversation about life.

Jason then changed the subject to what my plans were in the city. I told him about how messed up my day was so far and so the only plans I had remaining were business. He excused himself for a minute. A few minutes later, a flight attendant came over to me and handed me a bottle of wine. I asked what this was for, and she said, "Jason told all of us up front what a bad day you are having and we wanted to give this to you as an apology." While I was very impressed and grateful, I declined. A few minutes later, Jason came and sat back down.

"Thank you for getting her to offer me a bottle of wine, I really appreciate it."

"No worries, sorry about your long day."

Over the next several minutes, we shared a couple more beers, but Jason stopped at 8:00 p.m. FAA rules state that a pilot cannot drink twelve hours before they fly. As this point, our conversation turned to family. I spoke of my wife and two kids. Jason talked about his new wife and his son. We spoke about dreams for our kids, places we wanted to go and see, and what the next few years looked like for the two of us. Jason told me he was only flying tomorrow because he changed flight schedules with one of his pilot friends. He changed schedules so he could take his new wife to Europe in a few days to celebrate their anniversary. Jason spent a great deal of time talking about how he met his wife and all of their plans. I remember thinking to myself the woman he married was a very lucky person as it was obvious Jason was madly in love with her.

He then started to talk about his son, Matt. He spoke about trips they had been on together and some things they wanted to do. Jason told me he had to be a little careful of what he planned as Matt has a severe case of epilepsy and his day-to-day status changes a lot.

I could feel the emotion in Jason's voice when he spoke about Matt. I remember thinking to myself, *what if this happened to one of my kids?* You never think about something negative happening to your kids—as a parent, I only dream of what they will be like. I had never dreamed about something like a health issue standing in the way of my kids having an amazingly successful life. Who would? Jason was the dad that all of us dads want to be. He was going to ensure Matt's life was as full as it could possibly be no matter the physical challenges that were in the way. Jason spoke of seizures, medicines, monitoring—all of the things that most of us, as parents, don't have to deal with. Jason spoke of them like he was simply helping Matt with homework. He had a very surreal approach to it, almost an "it is what it is" attitude toward it. Even with all of the health issues going on, Jason and Matt still wanted to make plans to go see life.

Jason talked about wanting to go to a NASCAR race and shared a very personal moment with me that he and Matt had earlier in the day. Before Jason headed to the airport to get on the flight, Jason asked Matt a very powerful and emotional question.

"Matt, if your life were to end tomorrow, what do you want to do today?"

Jason said Matt never hesitated and said, "I want to go to a NASCAR race and I want to meet Jeff Gordon."

In my role at ADP, I sell software to the automotive industry, more specifically, to the collision industry, such as, body shops, where you would take your car to get repaired after you were in a wreck. As I said before, I was enjoying a fantastic career with a lot of success. I worked my way up to being one of the best sales people on our team and I was rewarded very well from a monetary and free trips stand point. In addition, I networked very well in this role and knew a lot of people within the industry. These relationships carried over to meeting and getting to know many people within the NASCAR industry. 2001 just so happened to be the same year that a new NASCAR track was having their inaugural race in Kansas City. A few months prior to the first race, I received permission to have a sales promotion within my territory. It was a pretty simple promotion. Buy "X product" and you get two tickets to the first NASCAR race in Kansas City. Being a NASCAR fan, I was very excited to be running this promotion.

To be honest, I promoted and marketed these tickets for my own benefit. Sales equal commissions and higher sales means an amazing free trip. The top sales people at ADP got to go on a trip of a lifetime as a reward for the sales year they just had. The trip, this particular year, was to the British Virgin Islands. There was no way that I was not going to take my wife on this trip. Even more selfishly, I ran this promotion so I could attend the race in Kansas City. How many times would I get to go to a "first ever NASCAR race" at a new track? I was pumped up. I was told I could distribute forty tickets to the race. I ran my promotion effectively and well. With just three weeks before the race, I only had two tickets left to hand out. For the life of me, I could not get rid of the last two tickets. I had really come to the conclusion that I was going to have to eat these tickets, give them away or something. Either way, the tickets were not going to the winner of the promotion I was running at the time.

When Jason told me about the conversation he had with Matt about where Matt wanted to go to next, I knew who would receive the two remaining two tickets. When I offered the tickets to Matt and him, Jason accepted

> ...we worked out the details to get the tickets to him...

the tickets with a big smile. While I physically did not have the tickets with me on the flight, we worked out the details to get the tickets to him and we arranged to visit with each other in about a week or so. I told Jason I could only make half of his dream come true, and that I could not get a meeting with Jeff Gordon. I went on to tell him I hoped this helped to achieve at least a little part of the dream.

When our flight was about to land in Newark, the pilot came on the radio and said there would be a slight delay in our landing as flights were backed up due to a fire earlier in the evening at one of the terminals. Jason looked at me and said, "Well, your day just keeps getting better and better doesn't it?" It was 9:45 p.m. when we landed. What a long day! When I got into a cab to take me to my hotel, the cab driver told me he had to take an alternative route due to the fire earlier at the airport. According to my cabby, flights had been impacted all day due to the fire. He told me several flights were canceled and so I should feel lucky I got into town when I did. My cab ride to my hotel in Lower Manhattan took me right past the World Trade Center. I remember driving past the two buildings, looking up and thinking to myself, *Holy cow these buildings are so tall.* I told the cabby the towers were so much bigger than I ever thought they would be. He told me I should take a tour of them someday. The view from the top is amazing.

# Chapter 3
## September 11

My September 11th started out like a normal day. Up early, a quick jog to start off with, a shower then get ready for my meetings. A group breakfast was next, with all of my friends telling me about the fun I missed in the city the day before.

At 7:45 a.m. I was in our meeting room, still catching up on stories from the night before with some of my peers. At 8:00 a.m. our meetings started. At 8:55, a hotel worker came into our room and told one of my managers of a plane crash into the World Trade Center. The manager decided to stop our meetings so he could check with our travel department as several of my peers were some of the people who had their flights canceled the night before because of the fire at Newark Airport. He wanted to make sure we did not have anyone on the flight that had just crashed into the North Tower.

Being a guy from the Midwest who lives in an area that has a lot of tornadoes, when our local TV breaks into regularly scheduled programming to tell us there is a tornado approaching where I live, I go outside to see if I can see the tornado. I know it doesn't make any sense, but that's what I do. When I heard an airplane crashed into the Twin Towers, I went outside to look at the tower since it was just down the street. I wanted to see it. I wanted to see if I could see the tornado coming down the street.

I went outside, looked up at the smoke coming out of the building and remember looking straight up and thinking to myself *how are those people going to get out?* I thought the people inside the building on the lower floors would be okay, but I thought the people on the upper floors were in a world of trouble. I watched for just a couple of minutes and decided to go back into the hotel to call my wife to tell her I was okay, that the plane crash was not that close to me, and I was fine. I grabbed my phone, looked at it to dial the number and the screen on my phone read 9:03 a.m. I started to head into the hotel when I heard one of my friends scream, "Look!!" I turned around and saw an airplane slam into the South Tower. The explosion was the most amazing thing I had ever seen in my life. I could feel the impact, I could feel the heat and the sound was almost deafening. My heart sank and immediately my eyes started to fill up with tears. My hand was in front of my mouth and the tears started streaming down my face.

> I turned around and saw an airplane slam into the South Tower.

At this point, I realized, as the entire world did, that the first plane was not an accident. I knew America was in trouble and I knew this was going to be a life-changing day for the entire world. I watched both towers burning and smoldering for a few seconds then bolted to my room to call my wife. When I got to my hotel room, my cell phone did not work. I tried to make a call using my company calling card, but that didn't work. The hotel phone did not work. I tried to get online to send an email. No luck. I ran back down to the lobby to use a pay phone— they were not working either. I ran back outside to see if I could get cell coverage on the street. When I got outside, people were running and screaming. Pure panic had set in after just a few short minutes. All I could see were people running, with fear in their eyes, with no sense of direction, no idea what to do, and no idea where to run. You could feel the fear in the air.

I stood for a minute and started crying again. The tears this time were not for what I was looking at, but selfishly, the tears were for my own fears. I was alone in the biggest city in the world with no lines of communication back home. I was alone, all I wanted was to be home, and I was scared. For the first time in my life, I was truly scared.

After a few minutes of watching everything, a friend of mine came up to me and told me we were going to get back together as a group and try to figure out our next steps. We got back together and held a private moment of silence for what was going on. They wanted to move forward with the scheduled meetings. I did not feel right. I was thinking to myself, *why are we getting back together with everything that is going on?* We did not need to have these meetings given what was going on outside our hotel. When we started the meetings again, one of the managers told us that one of the activities they had planned was to bring in an African rhythm band to teach us how to be in rhythm with each other all of the time. Each of us would be put into separate percussion groups of the band to promote unity among us.

To start with, being a white male over six-feet tall, I don't have a lot of rhythm. Knowing what was going on outside of the hotel room I was in—I did not have a heart to try to find any rhythm either.

This group effort ended up being a train wreck and one of the managers told us if we did not feel like being a part of the meetings anymore we could be excused and go do what we needed to do. At this point, I still had not made contact with my wife and kids, my brothers or friends. All of them knew I was in New York City. I went to my room and sat on my bed for a minute to gather my thoughts. After about twenty minutes, I decided I needed a beer. As I recall, it was about eleven or so in the morning. I called down to room service and asked them to deliver a six pack of beer to my room. The woman who took my order told me someone would be up within thirty minutes with my delivery. After I hung up, I walked to the curtains in my room and opened them up to look out of the window. When I checked into the hotel room the night before, I had no idea

**For the first time in my life, I was truly scared.**

my room had a balcony that overlooked lower Manhattan, looking directly at the Twin Towers. I walked out onto my balcony and stood there for what seemed like hours. I watched and listened to fire trucks and ambulances trying to get through all of the traffic. The traffic—and I have no idea what highways or roads I was looking at—was backed up for miles. No one was moving and it seemed like nothing was getting through the streets. The only things moving were the people running away from the towers.

I went inside to turn on the TV for the first time since the planes struck the towers. At this point in the day, flight 757 had crashed into the Pentagon and Flight 93 had crashed into the field in Pennsylvania. After watching TV for a while, I headed back out onto my balcony.

I have no idea how long I was out on the balcony. I just stood there watching everything around me, trying to call home, and trying to figure everything out. All of a sudden, I could hear a roar, like thunder from a couple of miles away. It got louder and louder. I looked up and before my eyes, the South Tower started to fall. I screamed a lot of very bad words out loud and started crying again. My hands were on my head while I continued screaming, staring, crying and praying. I felt so hopeless. I remember thinking to myself, *How many people did I just see die?*

> I remember thinking to myself, *How many people did I just see die?*

For some reason, I felt the need to be outside. I ran out of my room and went outside. On the elevator ride down, I tried my cell phone again to call home—again no luck. When I got outside there was almost a silence in the air. It was as if the entire city stopped and no one was saying anything and all of the sirens were turned off for a second. Looking back at it, all of the sounds were probably drowned out by the sound of the building crashing and the roar of the dust and smoke driving itself through the blocks of Lower Manhattan.

Today, when I am telling the story of me being in New York on 9/11, I get the same question all of the time. "What was it like being there?" My response is always the same. It was exactly as you saw on TV. I did not see anything differently than you did—except if you were watching it on TV, you could not feel the impact of the plane hitting the building. Your ears did not hurt when the second plane exploded inside the second tower. When you were watching the events of 9/11 unfold on your TV set, you could not smell the building burning. The sights, sounds and smells of the morning of 9/11 are things I think about every day and I suspect I will carry with me for a long, long time.

I stood outside for a while and felt the incredible need to be with people I knew. I did not want to be alone anymore. I wanted to be with people I could talk to. I went into the lobby of the hotel looking for any of my co-workers who happened to be hanging around. At first I could not find anyone and I found myself watching the TV in the hotel lobby. While watching the TV, the second tower fell. While I could hear the building falling, this time, I elected to not go outside. I had seen enough of the tornado.

About that time, a co-worker of mine walked up to me. He looked me in the eyes and asked, "How are you doing brother?"

I looked at him and said, "You know, I'm not so sure at this point." He told me several of our fellow sales reps were at the bar and I should join them. This sounded like a fantastic idea.

It felt good to be around people I knew. I felt a sense of comfort and security. For a couple of minutes, things were okay as I had many of my friends there. I remember looking around the table and seeing guys from Texas, Minnesota, California and Georgia. As comfortable as I felt, I remember thinking, *how in the world are all of these guys going to get home?* After a few beers, my friend who invited me to the bar said, "Hey Rob, didn't you fly into Newark last night?"

"Yeah, I did, why do you ask?"

"From what I am hearing, the plane that crashed into the field in Pennsylvania originated out of Newark and it was heading to San Francisco."

"What did you say?"

He repeated it.

When I heard him say it the second time, I jumped up from the bar and ran to my room as fast as I could and grabbed my wallet. I pulled out the business card Jason Dahl had given me the night before. Up until this moment on 9/11, I had not once thought of Jason Dahl. I sat on my bed and looked at his card for over an hour. There was an amazing battle of emotions and thoughts raging inside me. If I called and he did not answer, I knew it would not be good. If I called and he answered, what would I say? If I called and he did not answer and I got his voicemail, maybe his phone battery just died...that could be a possibility, right? If he did not answer, maybe the airport he was stuck in had no cell reception. That could be a reason why he did not answer. All sorts of thoughts, questions, and concerns were going through my head. The reality of it is, I was sure my new friend Jason was involved in the events that took place today and I was trying to ignore reality and come up with excuses as to why he would not answer if I called.

I walked out onto the balcony of my hotel room. By this time, the sun's shadows were starting to stretch out over the city. As I said, both towers were down by now, and the American Express building had fallen, too. As far as I could tell, the same cars were still in front of my hotel. None of the traffic moved at all. It seemed like the same fire trucks and ambulances I saw hours before were still stuck in traffic. I am sure they were different, but still, nothing was moving. There were less people on the streets running away from Ground Zero, but there were still some people walking away from the area. I looked directly down on the street below my hotel and saw a young woman holding what looked like a four-year-old little girl. I assumed she was the child's mother and she was covered in a gray dust; the same gray dust all of us saw on people exiting the towers. The little girl was crying and holding on to the woman. The woman was crying and trying to comfort the little girl. I never wanted to be home so badly in my life. I missed my family and I just wanted to get home. I looked across the horizon at the most beautiful city in the world, then I looked down at the streets in front of me. I felt so hopeless. I felt like there was nothing I could do. I looked down at the business card in my hand.

About that time, my cell phone started to buzz, communications were suddenly restored. My voicemail inbox was full of voicemails and text messages. I did not check any of the messages. I

> **I looked across the horizon at the most beautiful city in the world... I felt so hopeless.**

immediately called home. My wife answered and I immediately started to cry. Her voice sounded like a piece of heaven. It felt so good to hear her say something as simple as, "Hello." We cried together for what seemed like hours, but the only thing I remember from the conversation is when she told me about what our daughter was saying.

She told me that my daughter Abigail kept asking "Is that Daddy's airplane on TV?" I cried even harder. I never wanted to be home so badly in my life. I told my wife I could not remember if I told her, my daughter, Abigail, or my son, John, that I loved them before I left. I told her that I could not remember if I hugged and kissed everyone before I left. She told me I did and all of them know I love them more than anything in life.

We spoke some more, then I told her the story about the pilot I got to know the night before. She asked me if I thought the pilot I met the night before was involved in this whole thing. I remember saying that I pray to God not, but I think so. She told me I needed to call him to find out. I told her I was scared. She asked me what I was afraid of. I told her I was afraid of facing reality. She talked me into calling Jason and right before we hung up, I told her I would call her later, after I called Jason.

When I hung up, I noticed my message light on my hotel phone was flashing. I called the front desk and asked what the message was for. The woman at the front desk told me they tried to deliver the six pack of beer that I ordered several hours ago, but I was not in the room so they couldn't deliver it. I told her to send it back up.

A few minutes later a Middle Eastern man came to my door to deliver the beer. There was an awkward few seconds of silence between us. By this time, all of the major media and national networks were saying that Osama Bin Laden was behind the attacks on America and there were already talks of war against certain parts of the Middle East.

"Looks like you need a few beers, Mr. Quillen," he said just in time to break the silence.

"Yes, I do my friend, please come in," I said.

I invited him into my room and he had me sign the room service ticket. I asked him how he was doing, and he said he was scared. I asked him what he was afraid of. He told me he was afraid of what was going to happen to his family and fellow countrymen back home as a result of what we both witnessed today. I asked him where he was from he told me he was from Iraq. I told him I didn't think he had anything to worry about. He went on to tell me how scared he was. He told me he thought the attacks on America that happened today would start a large war in the Middle East and he thought America would eventually attack Iraq. While I tried to convince him things would be all right for him, his foresight was much better than mine.

I really should not put this into the book, but my new room-service friend and I shared the six pack of beer. I am quite confident that if he is still employed at the same hotel and his superiors read this, he would be fired. After all, drinking while on duty is somewhat looked down upon in this country. We went out onto my balcony with our beer, stood, and looked at everything below us. After a few minutes of silence, he said "It's a beautiful city isn't it?"

He looked over at me and saw the tears rolling down my face.
"What's troubling you, Mr. Quillen?" he asked.

"I miss my family and I think a friend of mine was one of the pilots on one of the airplanes that crashed today," I said, as I never made eye contact with him while answering.

"Do you have children, Mr. Quillen?"

"Yes, I have a daughter and a son."

"What are their names?"

"My daughter's name is Abigail and my son is named John Fitzgerald."

"After the president?" he asked.

"Yes."

"That is a strong name to name your son, Mr. Quillen. You should be very proud of him," he said in his thick accent.

"He is young, but I am very proud of him already. I can tell he is going to be a special person when he gets older. I can just feel it."

"By chance, do you know the meaning of the name Abigail in the Bible?" he asked.

"No, I don't, what is it?" I said, as I looked him in the eye.

"It means Fountain of Joy for a father. In your language, it means her father's joy."

"Well, I guess I got the name right for her then," as more tears ran down my face.

"I must go, Mr. Quillen. I thank you for your hospitality and I wish you only the best on your journey back home. I will pray for you and your family tonight."

Before I knew it, he left my room and I didn't have a chance to say another word. I drank a couple more beers out on the balcony while watching the chaos and madness continue to unfold in front of me. I looked at the business card from Jason Dahl again. It was now or never. I had to make the call.

When I was dialing the number to Jason's cell phone my hands were shaking badly. I was so scared to make the call, but I knew I had to make it. I entered his cell phone number into my cell.

The call went directly to voicemail. When the "leave your message at the beep" landed in my ear, my heart sank and more tears poured from my eyes. I will leave out the message I left for Jason on his voicemail, but I will tell you I wished him God Speed and I was thinking about his family, especially Matt, and I wanted and hoped to hear from him soon.

On 9/11, I stayed up almost all night. I called everyone I knew and told them I loved them. When I finished calling people, I went back out onto my balcony. I stared at the amazing dust and smoke clouds where the Twin Towers once stood. I watched countless fire trucks drive to the scene. The smell of death was overwhelming. If there was anything amazing about the view I was looking at, now that the Twin Towers were gone, now that the landscape had changed, it was the very clear view of the Statue of Liberty from my hotel room. I remember thinking to myself, "America is still standing."

The next morning, I went to the hotel lobby to eat some breakfast. I got off the elevator and walked toward the restaurant. I turned the corner and saw my Middle Eastern room service friend from the night before. We made eye contact and I smiled as he approached me. As he got closer, he put his hand out to shake my hand. I didn't put my hand out in return. When he got close to me I embraced him for several seconds. When we ended our hug, we both looked at each other and had tears in our eyes. He asked how I was going to get home. I told him I was not sure. I asked him if he reached out to anyone in his family back home, and he said he tried but had no luck. I told him that his family is sacred and he should never ever take them for granted. We embraced again, both of us with tears in our eyes and ended the moment with him telling me, "Shalom my friend, Shalom." He walked away and I have not seen him since. I think of him often, and I pray for him and his family. To this day, I hope they are safe.

# Chapter 4
## September 13

After watching New York City from my window for a couple of days, ADP thought it would be best for me to head to Manchester, New Hampshire, so I could get a flight home. They booked a flight home for me from there. The thought process was that if Manchester was the first airport the U.S. Government was going to open up following 9/11 to let fellow American citizens stuck in other countries back into the U.S., it would be the first airport to have outbound flights. In my mind, this was a great thought. I caught a ride up to New Hampshire with a fellow ADP sales rep who happened to live in the area. When my travel group made my flight arrangements they rented a car for me in case I needed to get around town during the couple of days I would have to stay in Manchester before my flight home. My friend drove me to the airport to get my car, then I headed to my hotel.

The next morning, I spent countless hours watching TV and checking with the airline to see if my flight was still scheduled to leave at 9:15 a.m. I was so restless, I just wanted to get home. I could not sit still in my hotel room. I could not sleep, and I could not watch any more TV. I kept calling home and talking with my family. I am confident my wife was getting sick of me calling and asking what the kids were doing. Each time I called, I promised my wife I would be home very soon.

On what I thought would be just another call home to check in I received the most heartbreaking news ever. My wife told me my new pilot friend, Jason Dahl, was the Captain of United Airlines Flight 93, which had crashed into the field in Pennsylvania. She saw his name scroll across the bottom of the TV. Even though, in my mind, I already knew it, TV confirmed he died on 9/11. I did not say anything for a few minutes and she asked if I was still there. I told her I was and she asked if I heard what she said and she told me again. This went on for another fifteen minutes or so. She asked if I was there. I mumbled something. She told me again then I started to cry again. I finally came to the realization that my new friend, Jason Dahl, was lost forever.

I turned on the TV and saw the same thing. I saw Jason's name scroll across the bottom of the TV screen. It was the list of the people confirmed to have perished as a result of 9/11. Jason, along with 44 other people of Flight 93, had indeed crashed into the field in Pennsylvania. Each and every one of the people aboard Flight 93 died as heroes. Everyone on that flight will always be remembered. I often think about each one of them and hope that God is looking over their families.

While I was deeply saddened that 9/11 had just taken my new friend away, I was even more heartbroken that a wife lost her husband and a son had lost his father and best friend. All I could think of is the hurt and pain that the two of them must be feeling right now.

Just get me home.

# Chapter 5
## September 14
## The Thought Process Kicks In

I woke up feeling incredibly restless. I needed to get out of the hotel and I needed to get home. Knowing I was confirmed on a flight home tomorrow made me feel better, but I was still restless. I thought a trip out of the hotel and a venture into downtown would get my mind off things for a while. Since I was in Manchester for the first time, I decided a drive around town to look at some local sights, knowing it would do me some good. I drove around for about thirty minutes before I realized I was the only one on the streets. The town was empty, stores were closed, and there was no traffic. The place was almost a ghost town. I drove around the town square again and I saw there was a sports memorabilia store open on Main Street. I went in and the guy behind the counter seemed stunned that I walked in. After exchanging hellos, I looked around. I found the NASCAR section and looked around for a while. I ended up buying a program from the NASCAR race at the New Hampshire Motor Speedway from a couple of years back that had both Jeff Gordon and Dale Earnhardt's autograph on it for $60. After all, Jeff Gordon is my favorite driver and earlier in the spring NASCAR lost Dale as a result of an accident on the last lap of the Daytona 500. I thought for $60 this was a good deal, something I could pass on to my son someday.

I drove around some more but found nothing was open and the city was sleeping. The trip out of my hotel was not helping much so I went back to my hotel and lay on my bed. I needed some time to think about everything that was going on. No TV, no music, no email…I just laid there…thinking. *What in the world is going on,* I kept asking myself. My head was spinning with thoughts, ideas, and confusion. After an hour of lying there, I turned on the TV and I saw the FFA still had not given the clearance for planes to fly again.

I got really nervous so I drove to the airport to see if I could confirm my flight plans for the next day.

When I arrived at the airport in Manchester, the scene was crazy. People were everywhere, I mean everywhere. Apparently, I was not the only one who thought this would be the first airport to open up. I stood in line for at least three hours and never moved forward. About that time, a representative from the airline I was scheduled to be on jumped up onto the counter and got everyone's attention.

"Ladies and gentlemen, I hate to be the one who tells you this, but we just got word it will be at least another two days before we start flying again. If you want to stay in line and make future travel arrangements feel free to do that. If you were scheduled to fly within the next two days, your flight has been canceled and I suggest you call our 800-number to see what your next best options are. I am very sorry....and God Bless America."

I ran as fast as I could to the car rental agency that I got my car from. When I got to the counter, I told the young lady helping me I already had a car rented from them and I am taking it to Lincoln, Nebraska. She looked at my rental agreement, then looked me in the eyes and said, "Get home to your family and drive safe." I called my wife and told her I was going to drive home and I promised I would be home sometime on Saturday night. Come hell or high water, I will be home on Saturday.

After getting back to my hotel room to pack my bags and gather my things, I realized it was 3:30 in the afternoon and I had just promised my wife that I would be home tomorrow. I logged on to the Internet and mapped out my route home. Twenty-seven hours from Manchester, New Hampshire to Lincoln, Nebraska.

"I am not going to make it home," I said aloud.

I called home again and told my wife I was going to sleep for a bit—then just drive. I must have been too excited to get home as I only slept for about twenty-five minutes. So, I started driving. I made it to Syracuse, New York, and I was beat. It was about one or two in the morning when I rolled into Syracuse and checked myself into a beat up hotel just off the road. I tried hard to sleep, but I couldn't. I tossed and turned all night and finally, at 5:30 a.m. Saturday morning, I hit the road again. I had to be home before midnight. After all, I made a promise.

About 9:30 p.m. on September 15th, I was in Des Moines, Iowa, just a couple of hours from home when I ran into an amazing thunderstorm, heavy rain and a lot of lightning. I was full of Diet Mountain Dew, adrenaline and worlds of thoughts were going through my head.

Four days after 9/11 happened and hearing the confirmation of the death of my new friend, I started to think about everything. Why did I have to go to the New York meeting? Why was I the guy who got kicked off of my original flight? Why did I have to be bused to a new airport? Why did Jason change his flight he had scheduled for this week? Why did I wear a Jeff Gordon shirt on the flight? Why did I talk to the guy

I turned on the TV and I saw the FFA still had not given the clearance for planes to fly again.

next to me on the plane? Why did he open up and tell me so many personal things? Why did I listen? Why did I care? Why did I have to see the second plane come in? Did I really have to see the towers come down?

I had so many questions going around my head. I just took the last couple hours of my drive home to try and get my thoughts organized. After all, I do my best thinking when I am alone in a thunderstorm. Not being the smartest guy in the world, it took me the better part of four days after 9/11 to really put this thing together. For the first time since everything happened, I started to think maybe everything happened for a reason. Maybe it wasn't an accident I experienced everything that happened the last four days. Maybe I was meant to see and hear everything I did. Maybe I was put on that flight from Denver to Newark to meet Jason for a reason. Maybe

I was put there to hear the dream Jason had for his son, Matt. Maybe I should do something about it.

# Chapter 6
## Getting the Plan Moving Forward

I pulled into the driveway of my house and looked at the clock on the dashboard in my rental car. It was 11:57 p.m. I had kept my promise to my wife.

I walked through the door and embraced my wife for what seemed like hours. It was one of the happiest moments of my life. I checked in on each of my children and smiled at them as they slept. I have a bit of a history of waking my kids up in the middle of the night when I come home from a long business trip. As hard as it was for me, this time I let my babies sleep. As tears came down my face, I remember thinking it was the most beautiful thing in the world that I have ever seen—them both sleeping in the middle of the night. I felt so glad to be home, but so fortunate and so lucky at the same time. I was one of the lucky people who got to come home from New York City after the morning of 9/11. My wife held my hand as I looked over my babies and she whispered, "Welcome home, we missed you." My wife and I held each other for what seemed like hours. I was so happy to be back in her arms and it felt so good to be back home again.

## September 16

I woke up feeling mentally tired and worn out...exhausted. But I woke up already thinking about what to do with all of the information in my head. My wife and I had an amazing conversation about everything that happened over the last four days. We watched a lot of the tapes she recorded for me while I was gone. Later in the day, I told her what I was thinking about doing. I told her I was going to try to get Matt Dahl to the NASCAR race in Kansas City in two weeks. I told her I felt like I was placed on Jason's flight that night to hear Jason's dream for his son Matt and that I wanted to make it come true. She asked me how I was going to pull it off. I told her I was not sure, but I knew where to start.

I had recently befriended a guy by the name of Marty Smith, who is now the NASCAR Insider for ESPN. At the time, he was a contributing writer for NASCAR.com. I sent Marty an email and told him some highlights of what I had been through the last four days. I also told him what I was going to try to accomplish for Jason and Matt. Shortly after I sent the email, Marty responded back with a simple, "Call me on my cell phone first thing tomorrow morning."

## September 17

Marty and I spoke first thing the next morning and I told Marty that I just did not want Matt to go to the NASCAR race with me. I wanted more. I wanted the entire dream for Matt to come true. I wanted Matt to not only come to the race, but I wanted him to meet Jeff Gordon as well. Furthermore, I wanted Matt to have an amazing experience. I wanted Matt to go to the race, meet Jeff Gordon, drive a race car, and be in Victory Lane. Said differently, I wanted him to have the best experience in his life. Marty suggested that he interview me for NASCAR.com to see if we could get the attention of the people we needed to get the process started.

If you are not familiar with how NASCAR works, back in 2001, getting a fifteen-year-old boy inside a NASCAR garage and on pit road was not something that happened every day. Anyone can go to a race and watch from the grandstand. But, to gain access to the garage area and on to pit road was somewhat difficult. The first thing that had to happen was that NASCAR had to grant permission for anyone under the age of eighteen to be in the garage area. It is a safety issue more than anything else. Given everything that had to take place, this seemed like the easiest part.

Most NASCAR drivers are just like you and I—they work for someone else. When a NASCAR driver shows up at the track, he has a full agenda already planned out for the weekend. They have sponsors who demand some of their time at each track and all of the drivers have sponsor appearances they are required to attend. Also, many of the drivers have personal charities they spend time with at each track. When you mix all of that into a very busy race schedule of practice, qualifying, required NASCAR meetings and— oh, by the way, the race itself, there is very little down time for a NASCAR race car driver at any race weekend. With all of that said, the driver himself rarely has any input to their activities for the weekend.

When you are a three-time NASCAR Sprint Cup champion like Jeff Gordon (he won his fourth championship that year), everybody wants a piece of your time. Your demands are higher and appearance requests come in from all over the place. Helping Matt acheive his dream was going to be very difficult. If I was going to make this dream come true for Jason and Matt, I would have to get all of Jeff's marketing

> **Marty's suggestion of doing the interview for NASCAR.com ...was pure genius on his part.**

people, PR people, the people with Kansas Speedway, sponsors and NASCAR to see the story well before the race in Kansas City. If I were to get all of these people to know what I was asking for, all of them would have to see the story at the same time. Marty's suggestion of doing the interview for NASCAR.com for the entire NASCAR world to see was pure genius on his part. Marty posted the interview with me on NASCAR.com the next day. Along with my interview, I reached out to local media to help get the story flowing through the news channels.

## September 18

Still not in the mood to get back to work just yet, I got on my home computer and checked my personal email account. Keep in mind, email was not like it is today. Today, when we go into our email our ISP or Outlook automatically tells us how many unread emails we have. Back in 2001, we had to wait for emails to download into our inbox. I started to download my emails. Twenty-five minutes later I had over 100 new emails to read, all of them NASCAR related. A lot of them were from fellow NASCAR fans who read the story on NASCAR.com. They were offering support, great thoughts and words of encouragement. Some were from fans who offered tickets for Matt and I to go to various races.

I received one email from an individual by the name of Jon Edwards. I opened the email and quickly realized that this email was not from a fellow NASCAR fan. As I read deeper into the email, I learned that Jon Edwards is Jeff Gordon's personal PR representative. The email advised me that Jeff Gordon was made aware of the story and that Jeff, Jon and Rick Hendrick (the owner of Jeff Gordon's team) wanted to do whatever they possibly could do to make Matt's experience at Kansas Speedway the most amazing weekend ever. Jon also told me he had already reached out to NASCAR and the age requirement was waived for Matt in order to allow him to be inside the garage and on pit road all weekend. In the email, Jon also asked me to reach out to several different people within Hendrick Motorsports and The Jeff Gordon Foundation to get the process started. I remember thinking to myself, *holy cow, I may have got this story into the right hands and the thing may be going in the right direction.*

I jumped up from my computer and ran to my wife and told her everything was set up. I told her Jeff was onboard and I was talking to the right people to make Matt's weekend at Kansas a reality. I was so excited!

She turned to me and said, "That is fantastic, but what did Matt's family say about it?"

"What?"

"That's great you have everything set up with NASCAR, but is Matt's family going to let him come out to the race?" It was like someone had punched me in the gut. I was at a loss for words, my mind was spinning.

I responded with, "Maybe I should ask them if they are interested in going?"

I got so caught up in working everything out with NASCAR, it never once crossed my mind to contact Matt's family to tell them about, well, everything. I realized I had never even thought about reaching out to Matt or Jason's wife, Sandy, to tell them about my chance meeting with Jason and to let them know about the emotional conversation I had with Jason just a few hours before he died in Pennsylvania. I was so focused on trying to fulfill the dream for Matt I never thought about anything else.

> ...it never once crossed my mind to contact Matt's family to tell them about, well, everything...

*Simple enough*, I thought. I will call 4-1-1, get their number and talk to Sandy about what was going on. I called information and learned the Dahl family's phone number was unlisted. *No big deal,* I thought. I had Jason's business card. I could call his office and talk to someone right? I called his office, but no one wanted to talk to me. I was able to speak with one lady at his office and while she was very empathetic to what I was trying to accomplish, she advised me she had strict instructions to not discuss anything about any of the airline personnel who perished on 9/11. I quickly realized I was out of options on how to reach out to Jason's family.

# September 19

Eight days after 9/11, some of the local media started to react to the interview I did with Marty on NASCAR.com. I received a few phone calls to do more interviews. At this point, I think everyone and all of the media were trying to capture anything positive that could come out of 9/11. I agreed to a couple of interviews with local TV stations in Lincoln.

While I had already received the email from Jon telling me everything was in place from NASCAR and Jeff Gordon's side of things, there were a couple of other things going on at the same time. I still needed to get in touch with the Dahl family so they could hear of my efforts to get them to the race. My thought process was as follows. The more the story was on TV, the odds of someone from the Dahl family seeing it would increase. The more people who heard the story, the better Matt's experience during the race weekend would be.

While doing all of this, I had no idea if this was the right or wrong approach to everything. But this was my decision on how to get things accomplished. While ultimately everything was accomplished exactly like I wanted it to, man, did I get a lot of backlash for it. Recognizing the fact there are critics for everything in this world of ours, there were a lot of people who thought I was going on every TV interview I could just so I could be on TV and get the attention. My goal was never for me to be on TV, or for me to get an opportunity to meet Jeff Gordon, or for me to get the national media attention. I was never looking for fifteen minutes of fame here. My goal was to get the story on TV so a dream could come true. A lot of people lost sight of this and got caught up in criticizing my approach to making the dream come true. In spite of the growing criticism, I forged ahead.

I completed a couple more local interviews and it was getting late in the afternoon. Even though the tapings went well, my mind was never far from the thought of *how am I going to get in touch with Matt and his family?* I spent some time with my kids and put them to bed. I went to my computer and downloaded several new emails. Staring at my computer for about an hour, I started to write a letter. A letter to Sandy Dahl, Jason's widow.

I was just typing random thoughts, comments, memories, and stories Jason and I shared. I wanted Sandy and Matt to know everything we spoke about. If I would never be able to speak with Sandy or Matt in person, I wanted to put everything into writing so they knew what Jason had to say before the events on 9/11. While I will never share the personal comments I shared with Matt and Sandy in the letter, I put everything into the letter. I shared every detail of our conversation and every emotion I had since 9/11. I spent the better part of two hours writing the letter. None of it made any sense. It was a rambling wreck of words, emotions, and scattered stories. My mind was scrambled and I could not make any sense of what I was trying to say. After I finished the letter I saved it to my computer and left it at that. I walked over to my wife and asked her a very simple question. I looked her in the eye and asked, "If I died in a plane crash tomorrow, would you want to hear from the guy that I sat next to on the plane today?"

> In spite of the growing criticism, I forged ahead.

She didn't hesitate one second before she responded. Her response was simple, but it hit me between the eyes like a punch in the head. "Absolutely, without a doubt, I would want to hear from him."

"Really, why?" I asked.

"I would want to know what was on your mind right before you died. I would want to know if you spoke about me or our kids." This was an amazing statement to me, something I will take to my grave.

> I would want to know what was on your mind right before you died..

How many of us have ever thought about that comment? "I would want to know what was on your mind right before you died, I would want to know if you spoke about me or our kids." While I think this is a very, very true statement, how many of us have really ever thought about it? What an amazing statement. With the advice and the soul shaking comment from my wife, I went back to my computer and printed my letter.

## Thursday, September 20

I woke up to several hundred new emails and a ton of voicemails on my cell phone. The national media started to pick up on the story and I had a lot of requests for more interviews. Personally, I only had two goals for the day. The first was to overnight my letter to Sandy Dahl. The second was to have as many friends as I could over for the Nebraska Cornhusker football game scheduled for later that evening. My favorite college football team is the Nebraska Cornhuskers and on 9/15/01 my team was scheduled to play Rice University. Like all of the major sporting events scheduled the weekend after 9/11, the Cornhuskers game was postponed. The game was rescheduled to a Thursday night game, but with no TV coverage. I did not care. I wanted all of my friends to come over, have a BBQ and listen to the game on the radio. My wife was amazing. She made tons of calls and tons of people came over to listen to the game. I think I spent about 500 dollars on food for the BBQ, but I didn't care. I wanted everyone there. When the game started, I cannot tell you how many people were at the house, but it was packed with friends, family and neighbors. Everyone was there. There were a lot of hugs, tears and fantastic conversations. It was the first time I had seen all of my friends since I got home from New York.

It was an amazing event, but my biggest takeaway from the night was seeing my father-in-law walk up the steps of my deck right before the game started. For

> It was the first time I had seen all of my friends since I got home from New York.

the first time since I had known the man, we embraced and shared some very personal moments together. Among other things, for the first time in our relationship, we told each other that we loved one another. Before the game started, I dropped my package in the drop-off box by my house. I remember holding the package in my hand and saying a small prayer that my letter would help me accomplish my goal.

## Friday, September 21

I got up early and went online to track my letter to the Dahl family. The letter was in Denver and on a truck, scheduled to be delivered before 10:00 a.m. I downloaded more emails. One of the many emails I received was from Blair Kerkhoff, who was a sports writer from the *Kansas City Star.* In the email, he told me that he heard about my story and my efforts to get Matt to the NASCAR race in Kansas City. He asked if he could come up to Lincoln and do an interview. Of course, I said yes. Again, my goal was to get as many people to know about the story as possible. We exchanged a couple of emails early in the day and before I knew it, he said he was coming up to Lincoln that day to do an interview with me and he was bringing a photographer with him. I remember thinking, *that's great, but what do you need a photographer for?* When Blair and I were done with the email exchange, I went back online to check the status of my package. The letter I sent to the Dahl family had been delivered. My heart raced.

Later that day, Blair and a photographer showed up at my office.

Blair did a fantastic interview. He asked amazing questions and got as personal as protocol allowed. In all of the 9/11 interviews I did during or since the event—Blair was persistent, but very professional, all at the same time. He knew how far he could go and he never crossed the imaginary line. When the interview was over, Blair asked for a few pictures.

I dropped my package into the drop-off box by my house.

I agreed, but never understood why. Some of me holding Jason's business card and others of me in front of my car. At the time, I was driving a 1994 Red Monte Carlo with personalized plates that read "24 Car." Like I said, I am kind of a Jeff Gordon fan. When the pictures and interview were done, I still had no idea why Blair needed pictures of me.

When Blair and the photographer left, I quickly went to my voicemail and email to see if Sandy had reached out to me. I scanned through several emails and voicemails, but nothing from the Dahl family. I had thirty-six new messages on my voicemail and 118 emails, none of which were from the Dahl family. I was starting to get frustrated with no response from Sandy or anyone from her family. *Why wouldn't anyone respond to the letter that I sent? Was it really not that big of a deal? Was I the only one interested in this?*

I went home for lunch and told my wife I had heard nothing from the Dahl family and I was going to call Hendrick Motorsports and NASCAR and tell them that bringing Matt to the race was not going to happen. I told her I did not think that I was going to make this dream a reality. She told me I did not know that for sure and I should keep trying. She asked me if I had anyone tell me "no" yet. She looked at me, took my hand and said, "Don't give up, if it was meant to be, it will happen."

# Chapter 7
## Making Contact

After lunch, I went back to my office and decided it was time to get some work done. After all, my job was to sell software for ADP. They were expecting it and I needed to get back into the flow of things. In my mind, fulfilling this dream was over. It was time for me to get back to reality and start making money for my family. I tried to get back to work, answering emails, scheduling business trips but my phone constantly rang. I answered all of the calls. It was one newspaper after the other. I gave a few quotes here and there. Calls came in asking me to give an interview at the race in Kansas City. Other calls were about interviewing Matt at the race, and still others were about how the Dahl family was doing.

While giving the interviews and quotes this time, I had an amazing shift of emotions go through my body. Twenty-four hours earlier, I wanted to talk to everyone in the media and get the story out. Now that I had almost given up on the dream, I did not want to talk to anyone in the media.

The phone rang again. It was another newspaper wanting to talk. This call was lasting longer than I wanted it to and then I heard a beep in my ear—it was call waiting. I had no idea who it was, but I thought it was a great time to end the conversation. I told the reporter I needed to take this call and he could call me later. I answered the incoming call, "Hi, this is Rob."

The response I got was, "Hi, Rob, this is Sandy Dahl."

I don't know how many seconds passed before I spoke, but the first words out of my mouth to Sandy were, "I am going to do my best to not cry right now."

She responded by saying that she was going to try to do the same thing. Leaving out several personal comments between Sandy and me, we eventually got to the point where she told me she received my letter the day before but she could not get back to me as she was attending the memorial service for Jason.

Sandy received the letter moments before she left to attend the memorial service for Jason. Man, did I feel like a major jerk. I wanted a response to my letter and she was attending the memorial service for her husband who had just died on 9/11. The conversation eventually turned to getting Matt to the NASCAR race in Kansas City, now just over a week away. Sandy told me she and Matt would be delighted if Matt could go to the race. Our conversation went back to the letter I sent her and I asked her a question I was not sure if I should ask, but I needed to know the answer. "Sandy, be honest with me. Should I have sent you the letter that I did?"

"Of course you should have. Why wouldn't you have sent it? Rob, besides the conversation I had with Jason when he got to his hotel that night—you were the last person to have a meaningful conversation with Jason before he died." We shared several personal stories, and then eventually started talking again about getting Matt to the race and all of the details we needed to work out.

> "Sandy, be honest with me. Should I have sent you the letter that I did?"

When we ended the conversation, we exchanged contact information and I told her I would call her the next day to update the status of things. When we were about to hang up, I told Sandy I loved her and I would do anything I could to make this dream come true. She told me she loved me, too, and she was looking forward to visiting again.

Shortly after my call with Sandy, Blair called me with some clarifying questions and I told him Sandy and I had spoken and that things were progressing to get Matt to the race next weekend. Blair and I shared a personal moment together and he told me he was very proud of me for what I had accomplished. I told him what I was doing was not about me, NASCAR or anything else. This had to be done because it was the right thing to do and anyone would do it.

"I don't think everyone would do this Rob, I really don't."

"I hope that everyone would do this, Blair."

My wife and I stayed up late that night. The kids were sleeping and we, like most of America at this point, spent a great deal of time just talking. We talked about life, dreams, passions, hopes and goals. Before we knew it, it was well past midnight and I mentioned to my wife that Blair told me the interview he did with me was going to be in the Sunday morning edition of *The Kansas City Star*. We headed to the Internet and typed in KansasCityStar.com to see if the story made the cut. The Sunday paper was already posted online and the story did not just make the paper. It was the feature story on the front page of the Sunday edition of *The Kansas City Star.*

There was my picture holding Jason's business card in my hand. The headline of "Fulfilling a Wish" was the main story of the Sunday *Kansas City Star.* "I guess that explains the photographer during the interview," I said to my wife.

I turned to my wife and said, "I thought they were going to put this in the sports section."

"I think this is going to be bigger than what I thought it was going to be," I said as we stared at the computer screen.

## Sunday, September 23

My wife and I went to bed around 1:30 Sunday morning and just a few hours later I woke to the house phone ringing. I thought, *who in the world is calling me at 5:30 in the morning?* I answered the phone and it was Bryant Gumbel's PR firm wanting to know if they could do a live satellite feed for an interview sometime during the race next weekend. Still 90 percent asleep, I agreed, hoping to get them off the phone so I could go back to sleep. I hung up the phone and started to head back to bed. The phone rang again, again, and again.

I took the last call at 11:15 that night. I have no idea how many interviews I did that day. I had no idea what I had committed to nor what was in store next. I was so busy with phone calls that day I had to record the NASCAR race. After all, it was the first race since 9/11. About 11:30 that night I watched it. The pride of America was as full as I had ever seen it. I felt very proud to be an American on that day. The race was held in Dover, Delware, which is close to a very large military base. The races there bring in a lot of military personnel to each event. On 9/23, NASCAR celebrated the military folks who were at the race. It was an amazing sight. Dale Earnhardt, Jr. won the race. I remember him driving around the track with a huge American flag waving out of the window. As a former vet, seeing the American flag wave to celebrate America was very special to me.

## Monday, September 24

First thing Monday morning, I called my boss and told him about how many calls I received and what I had committed to do over the next week or so as we prepared for the upcoming NASCAR race in Kansas City. I was trying to ask him for some time off to get organized, but before I could come out and ask the question he told me he woke up yesterday and read my story in the *Dallas Morning News*.

"Dude, your story is blowing up. You are everywhere with this thing. You need to run with this thing and make as much as you can happen with this. This is pretty cool." He went on to tell me he had received phone calls all day yesterday too, but his calls were from our bosses at ADP telling him to tell me to take as much time as I needed to make this dream a reality. "Rob, I don't expect you to come back to work for the next month—just go and get this done. It needs to be done."

After I got off of the phone with him, my cell phone rang. It was from a coordinator with NBC. They wanted to know if it was still okay with me if *The Today Show* came to my house tomorrow to film the story for the Monday morning show. For some reason I don't recall agreeing to this the day before, but apparently I did. I told them how to get to my house and that I was looking forward to visiting with them. Shortly after that call, I got a call from NBC Sports asking if they could get a few minutes of my time on Friday at Kansas Speedway. After that call, I received a call from ABC News asking me to do a live radio interview. After that, I received a call from a NASCAR radio show asking if they could shadow me during the race weekend and do a live interview on Monday after the race.

So on and so on. This went on all week. It never stopped.

# Tuesday, September 25

About 10:00 a.m. there was a knock on my front door. About thirteen people were standing at my door, it was *The Today Show* crew. Camera people, make-up people and lighting people all filed into my house. Twenty minutes later they completely rearranged the upstairs of my house to get the best angles and lighting effects, whatever that means. Soon thereafter, there was another knock on my door, it was Bob Faw from NBC. He was there to do the interview. He explained to me what was going to happen today and for the rest of the week through Monday. "Through Monday?" I asked.

"Yeah, we are going to shadow your every move through Monday to get a story for *The Today Show*, The NASCAR pre-race show and a spot on *The Nightly News with Tom Brokaw*. You are okay with this, right?"

"Sure."

We spent the next several days talking about my night with Jason, what I saw on 9/11 and what I was trying to accomplish with the upcoming race weekend in Kansas City. By the way, if you have never had TV crews shadow you for a few days, it gets pretty awkward from time to time. While all of folks were very professional and never crossed any type of personal line, it is just weird. Ever go to your office for a minute with a film crew following you? Ever go to a restaurant in small town America with thirteen of your favorite media people walking in with you? Ever try to get your kids to sleep with a make-up artist or a lighting person asking you to kiss your kids good night one more time for a second take? It is just a little weird.

At the end of the interview, Bob asked me one question I will never forget.

"Rob, what made you do this?"

"Bob, for some reason, that night on the plane, I elected to ignore my normal flight routine of keeping to myself and I chose to start a conversation with a perfect stranger sitting next to me. I chose to connect to Jason. Then I chose to listen to the man. Then I made a decision to do something about it, plain and as simple as that."

In a later interview I did, I was asked the same question and my answer was pretty logical, at least I thought so anyway.

"I assume that if I were to die tomorrow, and if I had a fifteen-year-old son with a big dream, that someone would automatically pick up on that dream and make it happen for him." There was a lot of talk about both of my answers. Many (if not all) people told me they would have never dreamed of making this whole thing a reality and many told me they never would have even thought of it again. Each and every time I heard this answer, I really questioned their response.

I kept thinking to myself, *why wouldn't you do something for a fifteen-year-old boy whose father had just passed away? Why would you just let it go? Why would you wait to make this happen?*

A man I met, some fourteen hours before he died, told me a dream he and his son had. Once I put everything together, there was no question in my mind I was going to try as hard as I could to get it done. Of course, I wanted to do it, but in my mind I had to do it. It was my job, it was my obligation. Why wouldn't everyone feel this way? Wouldn't everyone *want* to feel this way? I spent countless hours thinking about why someone wouldn't do it.

# Wednesday, September 26

Everything was set for the Kansas race weekend. I received an email from someone inside Hendrick Motorsports that not only was Matt's grandfather coming to the race with Matt, but that Hendrick Motorsports was going to fly Matt and his grandfather to the race in their private plane. We made all of the final hotel arrangements and I got a copy of the schedule of events from Friday afternoon on. Later in the day, I received a phone call from DuPont, Jeff Gordon's primary sponsor. They asked if my wife and I would join Jeff Gordon for a private reception on Friday evening. All that I needed to do was to be in Kansas City Friday evening.

# Chapter 8
## Race Weekend

I arrived at the track about 10:00 a.m. Friday morning along with three of my brothers and my two best friends. At this point, my mind shifted to being a NASCAR fan again. Walking into the track and seeing the cars practicing, hearing the cars on the track, and smelling the fuel burning reminded me of the love I have for NASCAR. For about fifteen minutes I was simply a NASCAR fan. I forgot about Matt, 9/11, and the camera crews around me. It was awesome.

My cell phone rang and it was someone from NBC Sports wondering if I was at the track yet as they were ready to start doing some interviews. I looked at my brothers and friends and told them I had some stuff to do, but I would be back in a bit. I had no idea this was the last time I would see them until about 11:30 that night.

About that time a golf cart arrived, picked me up and took me to the NASCAR trailer where I was handed "all access" passes for the entire weekend. I was then rushed over to the NBC media trailers to start my interviews for the day. I walked into the trailer and was quickly introduced to Bill Weber, who, at the time, was the lead NASCAR broadcaster for NBC Sports. The interview took forever, not because of them, but because of me. The lights were so bright and it was so hot inside the trailer. I kept sweating and sweating. They had to stop recording so many times, it wasn't even funny. Later in the interview, when we got into the heart of the story, they had to stop a few more times, as I kept crying and they gave me a few minutes to gather myself. When I was leaving the NBC trailer, a very well-known and popular NASCAR driver was standing outside with his PR representative waiting for his turn to be interviewed. The guy who had picked me up earlier in the golf cart walked me out and said something to the driver's PR person. I did not hear everything that was said, but I heard something about an apology for running behind and keeping him waiting. About that time, the driver approached me and asked if I was the guy who brought the pilot's son to the race this weekend.

"Yes, sir, I am. Sorry to keep you waiting, but I am kind of a rookie at this interview stuff."

He grabbed my arm and leaned in close enough that his face was next to my ear. "Thank you for what you are doing this weekend. What we do out here, driving cars around for fun, is nothing compared to what you are doing. You should be very proud of what you have done and I have a ton of respect for you and what you are doing. If you need anything this weekend, let me know."

We shook hands and went our separate ways.

*Holy crap, the drivers know about what is going on this weekend,* I thought to myself.

My golf cart driver dropped me off at a particular gate where more NBC folks were to meet me. Several interviews later, it was time for me to get back to my hotel to shower and get ready for our reception with Jeff Gordon. Right before I left the track, my cell phone rang again. It was a PR person from Jeff Gordon's group telling me Matt and his Grandfather had made it safely to Kansas City and they were on their way to their hotel. I smiled as I drove to my own hotel to get ready for my night with Jeff.

Jeff spent most of the night answering questions from fans, getting pictures taken and signing some autographs. It was then my time to get to spend some time with Jeff.

"Hi, Jeff, my name is Rob Quillen."

"I know who you are, Rob. It's great to finally meet you."

*Jeff Gordon knows who I am,* I thought. I must have thought this several times in my head where there was a strange moment of silence. Before I realized I had not introduced my wife to Jeff, he turned to my wife and introduced himself to her. "Sorry about that," I said to both my wife and Jeff.

We shared a brief conversation about Jason and Matt. There seemed to be a mutual appreciation between us for both of our roles during the weekend. When we were ready to leave, Jeff asked if I wanted him to sign anything for me. "You know what Jeff, this weekend is not about me. It is about Matt and Jason. Any other race weekend you would be signing everything I own that has the No. 24 on it. But tonight, I just wanted to say thank you for what you are doing for Matt. You are making several dreams come true. For this, thank you again, Jeff."

"No, thank you, Rob. Thank you for bringing this story to me." As we shook hands one more time, I walked away knowing that Matt was in great hands for the weekend. I left the room with a big smile on my face.

## Saturday, September 29

The morning was all about local interviews. Local TV stations from Omaha, Lincoln, and Kansas City had all scheduled times to visit with me. Luckily for me, I was smart enough to not schedule any interviews from 1:00 p.m. on so I could watch the NASCAR Nationwide Series race. I was very excited as I finally got a few hours to hang out with my brothers and friends and watch the race. After the race ended, I had dinner with my friends when all of a sudden I got very nervous. Tomorrow was the day that I was going to see a dream come true for someone.

I headed to bed, but only slept a bit.

## Sunday, September 30

My wife and I were at the track at 7:00 a.m. as requested. A full day of interviews, the race itself and, of course, I finally get to meet Matt. About 10:00 a.m., we arrived at the start/finish line on the track where Matt and his grandfather were just getting into the pace car for a quick ride. NASCAR had arranged for them to get a private ride in the car before the race. The media around us was crazy. About that time, someone from NBC asked me to carry a "personal" camera so that I could videotape the meeting between Matt and me. I declined and said I wanted the meeting between the two of us to be personal with no media at all. Just then, the pace car pulled around and Matt and his grandfather stepped out of the car. One of Jeff Gordon's PR people invited Matt to come over to meet me.

Matt and I shook hands, I could see the tears in his eyes, he could see the tears in mine.

"Rob, I cannot thank you enough for what you are doing for me this weekend."

"Matt, you are most welcome. I hope you know that your Dad was so very proud of you and he loved you with all of his heart."

"I know he did," was Matt's only response.

> ... the pace car pulled around and Matt and his grandfather stepped out of the car.

We spoke for several minutes and we got to share some great personal moments together. I wanted more time with him but about that time the Governor of Kansas, Bill Graves, walked up to Matt and me. Someone introduced Governor Graves to my wife and me. After shaking my wife's hand, he grabbed my hand and told me I did a good thing this weekend and he was proud of me. While I wished I could have spent more time with Matt, the meeting we just had was not about he and I. Our meeting was about fulfilling the dream that he and his Dad had and not about each other.

"I did not do anything, Mr. Graves. The people you see around us did everything," I said pointing to all of the various NASCAR personnel and Gordon's representatives. Before I knew it, Matt was being whisked away to go to the next event. Right after that, the people escorting Jeff around told us it was time to head to the driver's meeting.

The driver's meeting before a NASCAR race is a mandatory event for all of the drivers and their crew chiefs. It is an opportunity for NASCAR to explain to everyone any special rules for the race as well as an opportunity for NASCAR to explain anything different that may be going on during the pre-race or the race itself. My wife and I went into the meeting and were asked to stand in a very particular spot in the room. The best part about the meeting was there is no outside media present. This is a NASCAR rule and for the most part the rule is upheld. This weekend they let a couple of the NBC folks in with cameras, but all in all, not a lot of media for which I was elated.

Being a NASCAR fan, this is the most exclusive thing any fan could ever attend. All of the NASCAR stars are in a very small room and anyone you stood next to could possibly be someone who is a "someone" inside NASCAR.

While we were waiting for the meeting to start, NASCAR star after NASCAR star walked into the room. Dale Earnhardt, Jr, Dale Jarrett, Roger Penske, Rusty Wallace, Doug Yates, and Ricky Rudd. Shortly after that, I saw Kansas City Royals legend George Brett walk in. He was followed by NFL legend Joe Montana. Then Jeff Gordon walked in; Matt was right next to him. I watched Matt and Jeff sit down next to each other in the third row waiting for the meeting to start.

The meeting started with some general rules and regulations for the race and then NASCAR President Mike Helton took the stage. When he speaks, you had better listen and listen very closely. He was speaking about the upcoming race when the lady standing next to me asked what my association was that allowed me to be in the driver's meeting. I started by trying to briefly explain who I was and why I was there. She quickly interrupted me by saying "Oh, I thought that was you! You are the guy who brought the pilot's son to the race today!" After a few more words, I quickly realized she was the PR rep for NASCAR driver Sterling Marlin. About that time, Mr. Helton started talking about Matt being at the race.

He ended by saying, "Matt, we are very sorry about your loss, but we are glad you are with us today." Short of a standing ovation, the room clapped for several minutes and tears were everywhere. Before I knew it, I had tears flowing down my face. My wife and I embraced. For some reason, this was the first moment I realized that Matt's dream was coming true. I did it.

I kept thinking inside of my head, *I did it, we all did it. We made Jason's dream for Matt come true.* For the first time in my life, I made someone's dream come true. What an amazing feeling. So many emotions were going through my mind, heart, soul, and body. I was so sad for Jason, but so happy for Matt. I was emotionally exhausted from trying to put everything together, but at the same time, trying to remain calm and collected through everything while so much adrenaline was rushing through my body. I remember how proud I was of myself for getting all of this done. I think, for the first time in my life, I was proud of myself.

On September 10th, 2001, Jason Dahl told me the dream he and Matt shared with each other only hours before Jason got on my flight. Twenty days later on September 30th, 2001, Matt Dahl was sitting at a NASCAR race with his hero, Jeff Gordon, and I was watching it all unfold before me. A dream really had come true. What an unbelievable feeling.

I closed my eyes and said a prayer to myself. *Jason, I know you are looking down on us now. I hope you are looking at this and I hope you are smiling for Matt bigger than I am. I miss you my friend, enjoy this moment. Thank you for making all of this happen.* I looked over at the PR person for Sterling Marlin, who was crying, too. The two of us embraced as she said, "God Bless You," in my ear. I cried even more.

Jeff, Matt, and my wife and I all left the driver's meeting together. It was time for Matt and Jeff to go to the weekly NASCAR chapel service together. This was not a place for me or any of the media to go. This was one last private moment between Matt and Jeff. I was more than happy to let them go and spend a few minutes alone together. After all, this weekend was about Matt.

Jeff Gordon went on to win the race. When Jeff drove the No. 24 DuPont Chevrolet across the finish line, my wife and I embraced and cried. "Well, that could not have worked out any better could it?" I said to my wife. While Jeff was pulling into Victory

Lane, Jeff came over his team's radio and said, "This one is for Matt."

Matt had the time of his young life up to this point. He not only got to meet his hero, but he got to go the race and hang out with his hero. He got a behind-the-scenes experience of what it is like to be a NASCAR driver for a weekend. As Jeff Gordon said, short of driving the No. 24 car around the track, he got to do everything he wanted. New friendships were formed and for a short forty-eight hour period a young man got to forget about the pain that was still so fresh in his heart and mind. Many, many details had to be worked out in order for Matt to come to the race. Several dozen people, PR firms, sponsors, media companies, and NASCAR had to organize a lot of things in order to get Matt to the race. If you want to talk about several amazing people doing what they had to do to make something very cool happen—everyone did it.

> He not only got to meet his hero, but he got to go the race and hang out with his hero.

To this very day, I will never be able to thank everyone enough for making this dream a reality. While I thanked Jeff Gordon and Jon Edwards a million times, I will never be able to thank them enough for what they did for Matt. I will always be grateful to them for making the decision to make a dream come true.

I will quote my good friend, Bill Weber, when he spoke of what was done to get Matt to the race. "Rob, you did not save a life on 9/11, but on 9/11 you made a decision to make someone else's life better. You fulfilled a dream, Rob..."

Maybe that is what I did. Maybe I did.

# October 1

Back in Omaha, between more interviews, I started to digest the past twenty-one days or so. I ended my last interview right after I was on *The Nightly News with Tom Brokaw*. After the news was over, I called my mom who, at this stage of her life, was on the losing end of her battle with several different illnesses. She asked me why I decided to do this. I told her it would break my heart to know that someone would die with an unfulfilled dream for themselves or for their child. I told her I heard a dream both Jason and Matt had and that I had to make it happen. She told me people die every day with unfulfilled dreams. I asked her why it had to be that way. She told me she didn't think most people take any time out of their day to even think about fulfilling a dream for another person. At the end of our conversation, we exchanged some very personal comments with each other and ended the talk with her telling me that she was very proud of me.

> ... it would break my heart to know that someone would die with an unfulfilled dream..

It was not long after this my mom lost her battle. To this day, my mom remains my biggest hero, strength, and beacon of light. I think of her every day and I miss her dearly. I think of the last conversation we had together when she told me most people wouldn't take any time out of their day to think about fulfilling a dream for someone else. I thought about that a lot.

*Matt Dahl and author Rob Quillen*

# Chapter 9
## The Realization

Over the next several days and weeks, I tried to get back into the swing of things, trying to get things back to normal. While things were getting back to as normal as they could be in the weeks after 9/11, my mind was still elsewhere. I was not thinking about 9/11. I was not thinking about Matt meeting Jeff Gordon and I was not thinking about the NASCAR race that I just attended. My mind kept going back to one question.

Why?

Why was I assigned to the meeting in New York City when I could have gone to the meeting an hour away from me? Why was I bumped off my flight and sent through Denver? Why did I wear a Jeff Gordon shirt on the plane instead of a suit like normal? Why did I engage with Jason that night? Why did I listen? Why did I care?

The more I thought about it, the more I started thinking about how this whole thing, this whole crazy amazing chain of events was more than just coincidences. Up until this point, my only thoughts were that everything I had heard and witnessed was to fulfill a dream for a perfect stranger. The more I kept thinking about it, the more I started to think—what if what I accomplished is what life is all about? What if life is about listening, connecting and reacting to as many people as possible? What if we connected to others on such a level that we could start achieving dreams together before it is too late? What if this is my role in life? What if this is what all of us are supposed to do? What if everyone did this every day? What if we don't?

Several weeks and months went by and I never really did anything with these thoughts, but they were weighing heavily on my mind every day. A few weeks later, a close friend of mine lost his brother in a tragic car accident. The man was forty-seven years old and left behind two young children. I visited with my friend after the funeral and asked him how he was doing. "Rob, I am a mess. My brother and I talked about doing so many things. We always talked about things that we wanted to do, but we never did them. We never got to do anything that we ever talked about....we just talked." This really hit home with me.

In a twelve-month period I knew two people whose life ended suddenly and both had something in common with each other. Both of these people left this earth with unfulfilled dreams. Both of them left people behind who wanted to share dreams with them. I started to realize I was being sent a message and needed to do something about it.

It was at this point that I started an experiment. I wanted to try something. I wanted to get as close to each and every person I knew, met and was associated with. And when I say close, I mean so close that I know what they have for dinner every night. I wanted to know everything about them. I wanted them to not just know and trust me. I wanted them to share their wildest dreams with me, but I wanted to see if I could get to everyone's "inner layer" of trust, comfort and gain their confidence as soon as I could to get them to open up and allow me to help them achieve their dreams.

Sounds easy, heck, I already did it once, how hard could it be, right?

I quickly learned that people guard their innermost feelings and personal thoughts very, very closely. The risk with all of this is getting too close to someone too fast or just simply too close for their comfort. Everyone has a physical personal space line drawn around him. No one likes it when a stranger gets really close to them physically. With that said, everyone has a personal space line drawn around their emotions and personal thoughts as well. I learned not everyone wants to open up and share their innermost thoughts with you. Some people just don't share personal feelings. Even though I failed a couple of times, fell on my face once, and got nowhere more than once, I know this will work. I did it already.

After realizing I was not going to get to know every person in the world and make every dream in the world come true and recognizing the fact that not everyone is going to embrace what I was trying to do and knowing that I could fail again, I set out to try my experiment. This time, instead of having an "I'm going to save the world" mentality, I set a goal for myself.

I think there is some sort of saying about goals that goes something like, "always start something with the end in mind." My goal was simple. All I was looking for was one person a month to engage in conversation, get them to open up to me and allow me to get to the inner layer of trust and comfort and then work my way into hearing their dream.

# Chapter 10
## Testing Begins with the Experiment

I was scheduled to go on a long business trip to Canada for a potential large sales opportunity. As a result, I had an opportunity to sell a tremendous amount of the product I was selling.

During my northbound flight, I decided I was going to use this business trip as a chance to try out my experiment. The risk was huge. If no one bought into what I was doing, I was probably going to lose one of the biggest sales opportunities I'd ever had. The reward was endless. If it worked, I was on to something. Not only could I use this approach in my personal life, I could use it in my business life as well.

Everyone working in sales will tell you that a buyer will buy from someone they like before they buy the product itself. I agree this is 100 percent true. I wanted to see if I could create a whole other level of sales—a level where personal goals and dreams are included in the whole sales process. In my mind, heading to this appointment, I was going to get so close to these people that if I was any closer to them I would be on the other side of them.

All of my sales trips, both foreign and domestic, begin with some small appointments and client visits. Then I eventually get to the big appointment. After a few days of sales calls and presentations on this trip, I finally got to my big appointment. I walked into the room expecting only a couple of key people to be there. Upon entering the room, I was introduced to the owner of the company, the CEO, CFO, CPA, COO and production manager of the company. *Stick with the plan Rob, stick with the plan Rob, stick with the plan Rob,* I kept saying over and over in my head.

How many times in your life have you connected with six different people you have never met before and made a huge impact on their life in a one-hour period? Personally, this was the first time for me. I would love to tell you I was as calm as a lake's surface with no wind, but I was like a duck sitting on a pond. On the water's surface, a duck looks like it is enjoying a nice peaceful swim across the pond. But underneath the surface, the duck's feet are swimming as fast as he can to get to the other side to avoid contact with anything. This is where I am when the meeting starts.

Instead of starting the meeting with my normal "my company this" and "my company that." I just started talking, asking questions and listening. Forty-five minutes into the meeting our conversation eventually migrated to business. Two hours later, I received a verbal commitment to move forward on my business proposal. Six hours later, we were all at an unscheduled dinner. Three hours after that, I was at a casino with the same people enjoying personal time with all of them, and by now, a lot of their spouses had joined us.

At one point in the late evening—or maybe it was earlier the next morning—I am not sure, but I remember thinking to myself, *I just convinced an owner of a company along with his entire management staff and some of their spouses to participate in an unscheduled activity and everyone is having the time of their lives, and they just met me today.* What an eclectic group of people with wildly different personalities all having a fantastic time because I got them to reach their inner layer of trust and comfort with me. We were on the same page. We each fully understood what both of our goals were. Not just business goals, but personal goals for making the deal work.

During our meetings earlier that day, each person in the room told me their goals for wanting to partner with my company and the advantage they would gain by

> **Not just business goals, but personal goals for making the deal work.**

using my product inside their business every day. Each person in the room had different roles within the company. As a result, each goal was very different from another. Furthermore, I explained how using my products could potentially provide more earning opportunities than they had thought of previously. The bottom line was that if we partnered together, their business would reach the level of success they had always wanted to achieve. Said differently, if we partnered together, their company would become the company they set out to be when they opened up the doors many years ago. Don't look now, but dreams were starting to come true.

A few weeks later, we signed a multi-year agreement with the company in Canada. When we were done with the signatures, the owner of the company and I shook hands and congratulated each other on what we both had just accomplished. He looked me in the eye and said "Rob, in my wildest dreams, I had no idea we could find a business partner like you guys to get us to the level of business we set out to be at many years ago. This is my company's dream come true and I am so glad it came before it was too late."

Maybe I was on to something. Maybe the definition of "fulfilling a dream" for someone does not have to be a "dying wish" dream. Maybe someone does not have to be on his death bed in order to fulfill a dream. Maybe this crazy thought of "getting people to their inner layer of comfort and opening up to me" isn't such a crazy thing at all. Maybe dreams can come true before it is too late.

> Maybe dreams can come true before it is too late.

On the way home from the contract signing, I recounted the chain of events and started analyzing everything. In my first experiment, I got as close to everyone as I possibly could so I could hear their personal goals for doing the deal as well as hear the dreams of the company. I connected, listened, and reacted to everyone involved. My mind went back to that pain-in-the-back-side question again. Why?

*Why did it happen again?* I kept asking myself on the flight home. Why did you have success with the 9/11 experience and why did this deal just happen? Why have I failed at closing other deals, but managed to close this one? Sifting through all of the thoughts and conversations in my head, a crazy thought popped into my head.

What if these two events in my life happened because I made a decision to do it? What if I helped achieve two very different dreams for two different people because I made the decision to make it happen? What if the whole key to this thought of "reaching the inner layer" of people came down to one simple thing? Making a decision to do it, sticking with it and not stopping until it comes true.

> What if these two events in my life happened because I made a decision to do it?

I think if you only take one thing away from this book, I hope that it is to make a decision to do something and don't stop until you complete the task. I firmly believe people "think" about doing a lot of things, but never go through with the action–they never decide to do it.

Go back to the example of my friend who lost his brother in the car accident. They talked and thought about doing many things together, but never did. They never did because they never decided to make it come true. What happened to them? When one of them died, a hundred dreams died along with him.

Think about me getting Matt to the NASCAR race and meeting Jeff Gordon. Do you remember the dream Matt had? His dream was to go to a NASCAR race *and* meet Jeff Gordon. I could have been very content knowing I had tickets for Matt to come to the race and watch Jeff. I could have been happy having Matt sit next to me when Jeff took the checkered flag and pulled into Victory Lane that Sunday afternoon. But that was not the dream for Matt. I decided Matt was going to have the weekend of his life watching the race and hanging out with Jeff Gordon. I decided I was not going to give up on this dream until Jeff Gordon called and told me he would not participate in what I was asking him to do. I made a decision to make it happen. Furthermore, I could have sat back and done nothing with the conversation Jason and I had on our flight to Newark. But I decided to make something of it. Thinking and talking about doing something are opposites of deciding to do something.

Here is the beauty of what I am talking about, you can do the same thing. I am not writing this book to tell you about some "superpower" I have. I am writing this book to get you to realize you have the same opportunities in front of you. It's right there in front of you; you just have to make a decision to do it. Getting to the inner layer of someone and making a decision to help them achieve a dream is something that is not exclusive to me. These two things are in you and everyone around you.

> ...you have the same opportunities in front of you.

The one thing that prevents people from accepting this challenge is that most people are not decision makers. Most people don't want to be the person who has to make the decision. It's simple; make a decision to make it happen. Whatever situation is in front of you, make a decision. If you never decide to do it, it will never happen. This is what separates realizing dreams whether it is for yourself, your family or for others. Make a decision to make things happen.

I was awarded the contract with the Canadian company not because I said the right things, but by making a decision to get to the hidden layer of six different individuals. I made the decision to find out what their personal goals and dreams were and then found a common ground to make those goals and dreams come true. I am constantly asked the same question from sales people, "What would you say in this situation? How would you answer this question?" The honest answer is, I don't know. This book is not intended or meant to teach you to say the right thing at the right time. The point is you have to decide you are going to make a difference in someone's life, then don't stop until it happens. I can't give you the words to say or tell you how to react. At the end of the day, if you are helping someone acheive a goal or a dream, the words you say are irrelevant. All of us have a unique way of speaking, listening and responding to people around us. You have to use what works the best for you.

My style of communication and reactions to questions are very different from yours. You have to find your own way of making it work for you. Every relationship you encounter is different and everyone will react differently to your personality and conversations. The two examples I used are to show that if you take the time to listen, connect and react to everyone around you and then decide to do something with it amazing things can and will happen. Helping someone fulfill a dream is a fantastic feeling you will carry with you forever.

Go back to the beginning of this book when I asked you to picture yourself sitting next to a loved one and you both know that you have twenty years left together. You are *guaranteed* to have another twenty years with that person. Think about the person sitting next to you. Find out what their dream is. If that person tells you, "I have always wanted to go to Tahiti," I am not telling you to write them a check, but start working with them to make their dream come true.

Get them actively engaged in making their dream come true. Ask them what is stopping them from going to Tahiti. If it is a financial concern, help them create a budget and figure out how much money they need to save. Help them research via the Internet the best time of the year to go, where to stay, what to do, etc. Get them engaged in the process of making their dream come true and hold them accountable to ensuring that it comes true.

When the person you helped is sitting on the beach holding a drink, you are going to feel like you are right there with them.

Making someone else's dream come true is the most amazing feeling in the world.

All you have to do is make a decision to do it, because if you don't another dream might be left unfulfilled.

I will end this by sharing my all-time favorite quote. It is a quote from Lester Thorough who is an economics professor at MIT, an author and an amazing public speaker.

*"If you do **not** try, you will fail.*
*If you **do** try, you might fail."*

Go and make a difference in someone's life today, as tomorrow may be too late.

Why wait?

# Acknowledgments

There are so many different people and organizations that have made all of this happen. For all of your efforts, thank you so much. I am sure that I will leave so many people off this list and if I do, please know you are a huge part of this experience and I cannot thank you enough. If I left you out, I'm sorry, but please know I love you and I thank you for everything you have done.

Going back to the Kansas race in 2001, I have to thank so many different people and organizations.

I have to start with KOLN TV in Lincoln, Nebraska. Thank you for being the first TV station to put this story on TV.

Thank you to Blair Kerkhoff with *The Kansas Star* for being amazingly professional during a very emotional time for me.

To NBC, NBC News, NBC Sports and NASCAR on NBC for not only being professional but for being so supportive in getting my efforts on the air to fulfill a dream for the Dahl family. Bob Faw is an amazingly talented reporter and I thank him a ton. Furthermore, Bill Weber, who is a professional sports anchor, was nothing short of amazing. Thank you for making pre-race time for my story.

To the family of David Bloom, words cannot express my feelings toward your loss. I hope all of you are well and I cannot express to each and every one of you my gratitude for David's love of my story. God bless you all.

Marty Smith, who made so many things happen to make this dream come true, you are an amazingly talented person who only reports through your heart. NASCAR should be thankful you are a part of a sport that so many people love. You will never know the love I feel for you brother. Thank you so much, man.

To NASCAR, where do I begin? Your willingness and efforts to make Jason and Matt's dream come true are still amazing to me to this day. You changed the rules and made things happen and that you didn't have to, but you did. For this I am eternally grateful.

Mike Helton and Becky Darby made a lot of things happen. For this, the both of you are forever in my heart.

Mr. Helton, you acknowledged Matt Dahl before the Kansas race and got all of the NASCAR drivers to see him, too. When you introduced Matt while he was sitting next to Jeff Gordon, I know his heart was full of emotion when all the drivers and crew members recognized him. I know he still carries that with him today. Thank you for doing this. As always, when you speak, your words are powerful even if they are received by a fifteen-year-old boy.

To the Jeff Gordon Foundation, I cannot put enough words on this page to thank you enough. Your efforts and the efforts of so many different people within the foundation were nothing short of amazing. You did everything you could to make this dream come true, and it did—thanks for all of your efforts. All of you are rock stars to me.

Jon Edwards, where do I begin? After putting everything into the media to make this dream come true, you were the first person who responded to my emails and calls. I am not going to lie to you, the night I received and read your email I cried. Your response was amazing, beautiful and I was so grateful. I cannot thank you enough. You made so many things happen and introduced me to a lot of different people who helped put everything into action. You were the springboard to everything happening. Since our first meeting in 2001, you have always been there for anything I ever needed. Thank you.

Of course, none of this would have happened if Jeff Gordon would have said no to being a part of this. Through the efforts of so many people whom I have outlined in this book and on this page, Jeff was the key to everything. Jeff, not only did you hear the story and the dream, you welcomed and embraced it with open arms. When you said yes, this book and its message took root. Thank you for making a lot of people's dreams come true.

To Sandy Dahl, words will never be able to describe how sorry I am about your loss of Jason. Your husband died an amazing husband and father as well as a hero to every person in America. Thank you for accepting me into your family and letting me be a part of The Jason Dahl Scholarship Foundation. I am so humbled to be a part of it. You mean the world to me and I would do anything for you.

Of course, I could not finish this without acknowledging my wife, Sue Anne, and my children Abigail and John. You have always been there for me. You have supported me and encouraged me to achieve all of my dreams. You will never know how much I love you and I cannot thank you enough for everything.

There are so many other people that I want to say thank you to. All of you, directly or indirectly have impacted not only my life, but this book and my speaking tour. While you may not know it, all of you have made everything happen for me.

Nancy and Jerry, ADP, Geneva State Bank, Don "The Rock" Hancock, John, Bonnie and Lacey Jo and so, so, so many other people. I love all of you and I will never find words to thank you enough.

A portion of the proceeds from this book go directly back to The Jason Dahl Scholarship Foundation, which is a foundation created shortly after 9/11 to provide scholarship dollars to high school and college students wanting to earn or working toward their aviation degree. This foundation provides thousands of dollars in scholarship money every year to so many deserving people. Please help me continue to raise money for this group.

Please visit the foundation's web site at www.TheDahlFund.org. If you can find a place in your heart to make a donation, please do so.

To request a speaking engagement or to read about my amazing publisher, please visit www.HeadlineBooks.com.

For more information about Epilepsy, please visit www.epilepsyfoundation.org. So many of us are impacted by this disease, let's work toward eliminating it.

To find out where I am and what I am doing, feel free to visit www.RobQuillen.com. This site is updated often and I blog as much as I can. You can also get more information about speaking appearances on the web site.

Feel free to follow me on Twitter @Nascartwodozen. If you want to catch up with me on Facebook, I always accept friend requests. Just search Rob Quillen and you will get there.

Thank you, thank you, thank you to everyone for making everything happen. All of you have the power to make someone else's dreams come true...just make a decision to do it.

I love you all.